Contents

Foreword..5

In a Nutshell 6

    Scales...6

    Chords..7

    Improvising...7

    The Pattern Trap 8

    Takeaway 9

In Depth..10

    Scales..10

        Filling in the Gaps...10

        4NPS Practice..11

        Here's One I Made Earlier 13

        The Mind-blowing Bit 13

        String Skipping 14

        Takeaway...14

    Chords..14

        What About Key Signatures? 16

        Takeaway...16

5 of Allan's 10 Most Useful Scales 17

    1. The Major Scale...17

    2. The Melodic Minor Scale 18

    3. The Harmonic Minor Scale 18

    4. The Lydian Diminished Scale 19

    5. The Diminished Scale 20

Two Holdsworthian Diminished Scales 21

Putting It All Together – How to Practice...........................24

    A Word About Technique..24

Putting It All Together – Making it Work............................25

Scale/Chord Reference Section..27

    C Major 27

    C Melodic Minor..27

    C Harmonic Minor 28

    C Lydian Diminished..29

    C Diminished 29

    G Major 30

    G Melodic Minor 30

    G Harmonic Minor 31

    G Lydian Diminished 31

    G Diminished..32

    D Major 32

    D Melodic Minor 33

    D Harmonic Minor 33

    D Lydian Diminished 34

    D Diminished 34

    A Major 35

    A Melodic Minor 35

    A Harmonic Minor 36

    A Lydian Diminished..36

    A Diminished..37

    E Major 37

    E Melodic Minor...38

    E Harmonic Minor..38

    E Lydian Diminished 39

    E Diminished 39

    B Major 40

    B Melodic Minor 40

    B Harmonic Minor 41

B Lydian Diminished 41

B Diminished 42

F# Major 42

F# Melodic Minor 43

F# Harmonic Minor 43

F# Lydian Diminished 44

F# Diminished 44

C# Major 45

C# Melodic Minor 45

C# Harmonic Minor 46

C# Lydian Diminished 46

C# Diminished 47

Ab Major 47

Ab Melodic Minor 48

Ab Harmonic Minor 48

Ab Lydian Diminished 49

Ab Diminished 49

Eb Major 50

Eb Melodic Minor 50

Eb Harmonic Minor 51

Eb Lydian Diminished 51

Eb Diminished 52

Bb Major 52

Bb Melodic Minor 53

Bb Harmonic Minor 53

Bb Lydian Diminished 54

Bb Diminished 54

F Major 55

F Melodic Minor 55

    F Harmonic Minor.. 56

    F Lydian Diminished 56

    F Diminished 57

A Final Word 58

More from Unlock the Guitar 59

Foreword

Ever since my first guitar teacher introduced me to the music of Allan Holdsworth in the late 90s, it has been an ongoing apprenticeship. I became fascinated, not only with his music, but with his approach to music itself, and the way he thinks about chords, scales and improvisation.

Allan's REH video was a blessing for me as I was able to glean enough insight into his playing to understand the way the great man thinks, and more importantly to begin to apply those concepts to my own playing. I struggled with music theory and orthodox approaches, so when Allan's beautifully simple way of thinking about chords and scales clicked for me, I knew I had found something that finally made sense.

I must admit, I couldn't play you a single Allan Holdsworth lick, and I wouldn't want to as the thought of dissecting his music in that way was always unappealing to me. What I wanted to do was get inside his head, grasp his way of thinking about music, and find out exactly how he was able to come up with such intricate yet outrageous lines and compositions. And that is precisely what this book is about.

Allan's playing looks incredibly complicated, and then some, to the innocent bystander, but the approach behind it is incredibly simple and easy to grasp. It's so straightforward in fact that most players who have attempted to describe what he does completely miss the point. Once you do understand his approach, however, you'll have a new appreciation for how far he's taken it, and how far it can go.

This book is not for the faint-hearted, but you shouldn't be put off by thinking that you'll be getting to grips with a lot of tricky concepts, because you won't; Allan's way of thinking is almost childlike in its simplicity, and when you glimpse it I can assure you that the light bulbs will come on!

In this book I go into detail on Allan's approach to chords and scales, as well as the salient features of his technique, should you wish to emulate the sound he creates. I've also included plenty of scale charts to be studied in the way Allan does in order to learn to improvise, as well as extract chords.

Let's get started!

Graham

www.unlocktheguitar.net

In a Nutshell

Allan is often quoted as saying that he doesn't like the guitar, and that it wasn't the instrument that he would have chosen. He claims he would have much preferred to be a horn player, and it is this disdain for the guitar that helps him see it as a mere tool for expressing musical ideas and compositions. If you see the guitar as a tool or a piece of wood with however many frets and six (or more strings) and a couple of pickups, you're unlikely to be motivated to want to emulate the guitar greats of your time. Holdsworth's taste in music leans more to classical composers such as Ravel, Debussy, Stravinsky, Copland, and Bartok, and jazz horn players such as Charlie Parker and John Coltrane, which can be heard in his obsession with getting a sax-like guitar tone; this also being the driving force behind his technique.

Scales

Holdsworth is an improviser first and foremost, and early on in his development he thought that to be able to improvise he'd have to learn every scale that went with every chord. He pretty much accomplished this, and this is the first key to understanding his playing: **scales come first**.

Holdsworth's first port of call for improvising, coming up with chords, comping, and composing are scales; he thinks in terms of scales. Where most guitarists would see a set of chords, Holdsworth sees a set of scales changing. For him the notes of the chords are part of those scales, rather than static chords or chord shapes in a progression. When the chords are going by he's thinking of entire scales the full length of the neck going by with the chords as merely parts of those scales. Think about that for a second... It should be somewhat mind-blowing. Let me show you what I mean:

In Holdsworth's mind a C Major scale would look something like this:

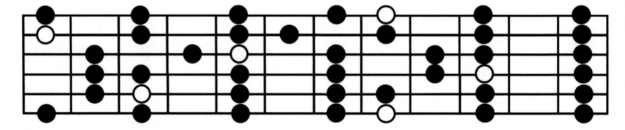

A bunch of dots 'lit up' on the fretboard, as he describes it. Now, here's the interesting part:

Chords

Any group of two or more notes played together from the above fretboard diagram is a 'C major' chord, or a chord that will work in a C Major tonality, such as these:

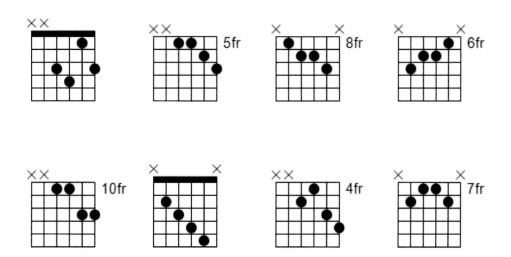

If you play through the chords, you'll probably find them a little 'melodically unstable', and this is because Holdsworth is not particularly interested in a set of chords which are nicely stacked in thirds for each key. He's more interested in the chordal possibilities that can be pulled from a scale pattern **on the guitar as a tool**, and once you start exploring these possibilities you realize that there's a lot of scope for creating chords from scale patterns.

Do you need to name the chords? Not really... And this is one of the strengths of Holdsworth's system: Since you know that all those chords belong to the C Major scale, you can use them as chords, substitutions or for improvising in a C Major tonality, safe in the knowledge that they'll work because they're all diatonic to C Major, however 'out there' they may sound. Names are not necessary as you're just grabbing parts of the C Major scale—the sound, on the other hand, is very much a question of taste.

Improvising

As for improvising, Holdsworth sees this scale as useful for playing over D minor, G7 and C major tonalities. He does not take modes into account, and actually describes them as a 'hindrance'. The idea, as he coins it, is then to 'juggle the notes around and come up with melodies', from your neck-long palette. What stops you being able to do this with any sense of freedom like Holdsworth does has nothing to do with the size of your hands; it's the way you've learned, or are learning scales.

The Pattern Trap

Holdsworth suggests learning scales in four-note-per-string patterns, and there are a couple of good reasons for this, which he doesn't go into.

The first is that a four-note-per-string (4NPS) pattern is not a pattern, nor does it create one in the first place, check it out:

4NPS Major Scale in F

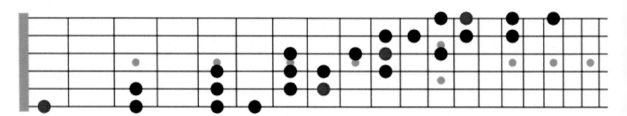

The second is that 4NPS runs force you to respect the, 'next note, next finger' sequence, which opens up your hand like Holdsworth's. Again, having large hands is not a necessity for this system because if you play three-note-per-string scales such as the one below, also in F...

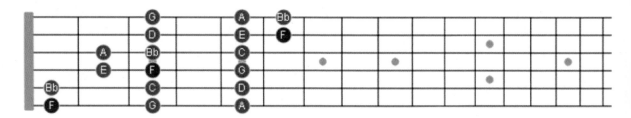

You'll notice that you probably play it with this fingering: 1-2-4, 1-2-4, 1-2-4, 1-2-4, 1-3-4, 1-3-4. In other words, for over half the pattern your third finger is just dangling there, and then for the B and E strings your second finger is not used. Again, you don't need big hands, you just need to actually use your whole hand!

Takeaway

-Work from the point of view of scales.
-Use your whole hand (next note-next finger)
-Forget about scale boxes; CAGED, 3NPS or otherwise.
-Forget about modes.
-Chords are simply parts of a scale, not neat sequences of stacked thirds.

If these concepts are new to you, take a moment to digest them before moving on as in the next few chapters we'll take an in-depth look at these ideas, and how far you can go with them.

In Depth

Inventing your own system to replace music theory is by no means a small order, but Allan managed to come up with a system that made sense to him, and that he is able to use to great effect in his writing and improvising. In this section we take an in-depth look at the approaches outlined in the first section by expanding on them and accessing them for your own use and playing.

Scales

It is clear from the first section that any kind of scale pattern or box such the 3NPS or CAGED system, and especially those pentatonic boxes, is going to be a major hindrance. You can probably see why if you've been experimenting, and may be wondering how you can 'undo' all those boxes and free up the neck. The good news is that you don't need to 'forget' or 'undo' anything; you just need to refrain from playing in boxes.

First of all, I'd highly recommend, as Allan does, playing through the 4NPS patterns. You don't need to memorize the patterns as what you're really working on here are the points mentioned in the previous section:

1) **Next note, next finger**. 4NPS patterns force you out of trailing/unused fingers as in the 3NPS or CAGED patterns. They are also a good way to stretch your hand without straining it.

2) **No pattern, no cry**. Your focus shifts to note location as oppose to the rote memorization of patterns.

Filling in the Gaps

Learning scales as Holdsworth sees them—the entire length of the fretboard—may sound like a daunting task, but it's simply a question of doing what you don't normally do to learn scales: play up and down one string or diagonally i.e. the horizontal approach. Most players confine themselves with vertical patterns which turn into 'fretboard blinkers' making it hard to see outside of the boxes. Simply avoiding playing vertically will soon open up the fretboard for you.

The scale reference section provides many fretboard diagrams to help you with this process. Each diagram shows all the available notes up to the 12th fret. Remember that the goal is to learn the location of the available notes within a scale pattern, not create a bunch of box patterns.

4NPS Practice

Use the 4NPS patterns below to practice. You'll start to make use of the entire span of your hand on the fretboard which may feel uncomfortable at first, and you'll also see past the patterns.

F Major

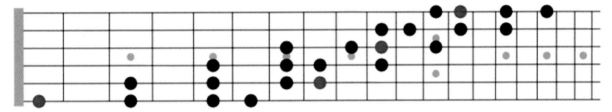

F Minor

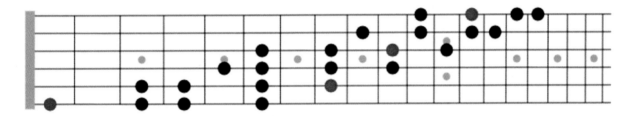

F Harmonic Minor

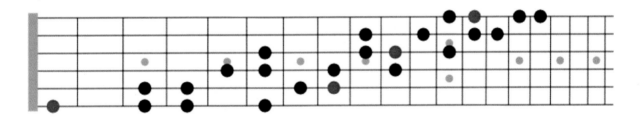

F Melodic Minor

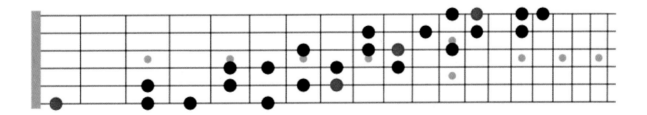

F Diminished

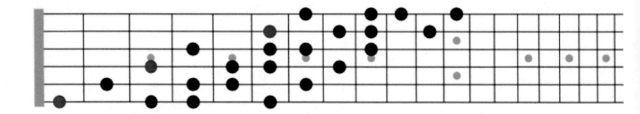

The following patterns are also 4NPS but start on the 5th string root.

Bb Major

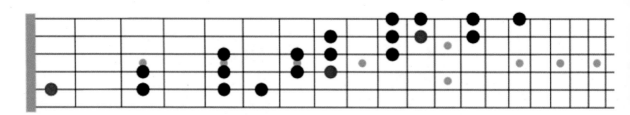

Bb Minor

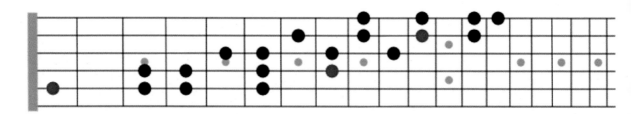

Bb Harmonic Minor

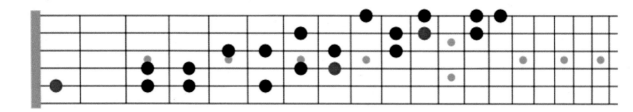

Bb Melodic Minor

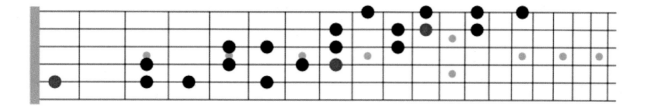

Here's One I Made Earlier

The diagram below is what you should end up seeing as your fretboard palette for improvising over F Major / G Minor / C7 tonalities. I find it easier to see the entire fretboard as two twelve-fret portions, or even two guitar fretboards (upper and lower); that way you can treat the 12th fret as the nut and simply superimpose the lower pattern on the upper frets. Incidentally, Allan's guitars are nearly always 24-fret models, which helps for this 'mirror' view of things.

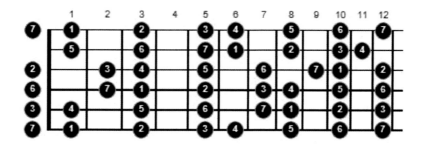

I've included the open strings that are available for use in your own playing, even though Allan himself is not a great user of open strings on the guitar. I imagine this is because the sound is too twangy for his liking.

The Mind-blowing Bit

While you may be used to thinking of scales as starting on a particular note, Allan does not really think this way. For him, scales are permutations of intervals that are more akin to circular shapes than a static series of notes with a defined starting and ending tone. Therefore, he's seeing the permutation of intervals as a circular pattern rather than modes or even root notes for that matter. This is a little hard to grasp at first, but chew it over for a while. To give you a little more insight into this way of seeing things, let's look again at a C Major Scale:

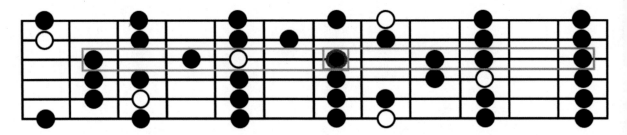

If you focus on the D note on the G string at the 5th fret, you'll see that the scale is symmetrical in both directions, and this is a device Allan used to memorize scale patterns. If you play up the fretboard using four fingers from the D note, and do the same going down, you've covered a lot of ground. To Allan, this would be a D Minor Scale with a natural 6th, although he is aware that it is also a C Major Scale.

String Skipping

As Allan says, try to force your fingers to go in directions they wouldn't normally go, so that you end up in parts of the fretboard that are probably gathering dust. This especially includes skipping strings and implementing that wider reach. If you haven't attempted string skipping before, it's quite an eye-opener as to how well you're digesting the patterns.

Takeaway

-Focus on learning scales in a horizontal and/or diagonal fashion.
-Vertical playing won't give you the freedom of the whole neck.
-Force your fingers in different directions using string skipping.

Chords

As previously mentioned, Allan's chordal playing is derived from scales, and in particular the way the notes fall on the neck of the guitar dictates the chord 'shapes' available. Allan does know 'standard' chord shapes, but avoids them as he finds their sound ugly and dissonant.

Allan's method of extracting chord shapes from scales is incredibly efficient due to its simplicity, and leads to infinite possibilities for comping and coming up with unusual chords you'd probably never have considered without a very advanced understanding of music theory.

If you were comping on Dm7, you would probably use the chord shapes you know; whereas in the Allan's system you could use **groups of notes from a scale that Dm7 is diatonic to** such as C Major. Here's a recognizable Dm7 shape:

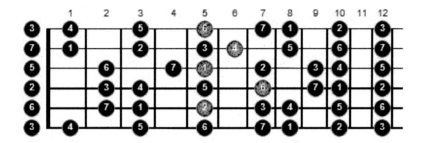

But you could also use these chords, according to taste, as they're part of the scale. Allan usually extracts them in sequences like this, going along the fretboard in sets of notes after finding a chord shape he likes.

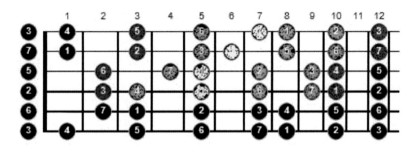

Dm7 is also diatonic to C Melodic Minor:

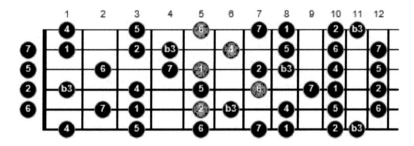

Here's a set of chords Allan might come up with for comping purposes:

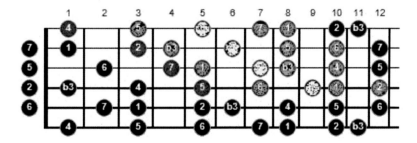

Again, any group of (tastefully selected) notes from the above diagram is also fair game for comping on Dm7.

In fact, if you permutate the scales that Dm7 could potentially belong to, you'll end up with more than you'd ever want to know about! But this is what Allan does—he pulls chords from scales—when he's comping. This process may seem complex, but it is actually painfully simple as long as you know the scale pattern well. There's no need to think in terms of names of chords, or do complex music theory calculations as you're just selecting random shapes that you know will work because they're part of the scale.

When you start to apply this process, you'll find that pulling out chords reinforces your awareness of note location, and practicing scales reinforces your ability to pull out chords, especially on the fly.

What About Key Signatures?
I don't think Allan considers key signatures when composing or improvising as he probably finds them too limiting. He also has his own notation system which is not based on key signatures. Moreover, if you're thinking in terms of entire scales changing as the chords go by, then key signatures become somewhat redundant and impractical due to the nature of the music.

Takeaway
-Use the 4NPS patterns to start using your whole hand.
-Forget about key signatures.
-A chord can be derived from any number of scales.
-In this system it is not necessary to name every chord you come up with.

5 of Allan's 10 Most Useful Scales

If you've seen Allan's REH video, there's a section where he goes through his 10 most useful scales for playing over pretty much anything. This begs the following question: if these are the 10 most useful scales, how many scales does he know?! I don't have the answer, but I imagine he knows a fair few more than 10 since he talks of working out all the permutations of 5, 6, 7, 8 and 9 note scales, then discarding the ones with more than 4 semi-tones in a row. What's more, if you think about the possible scales that contain the notes of a Dm7 chord, as in the previous chapter, it's probably a good idea to keep things to around 5 or so scales, which is still and incredible amount of material to work through.

Let's take a look at 5 of Allan's 10 Most Useful Scales.

1. The Major Scale

The example here is in C, and Allan refers to it as a D Minor, C Major, G7 scale which I imagine are the diatonic chords he associates with it. Allan also comments here that there are different names for scales starting on different notes of the scale (the modes), but that this was more of a hindrance to him than anything else. Allan also refers to this scale from the perspective of D with a natural 6th (D Dorian—although he never calls it this).

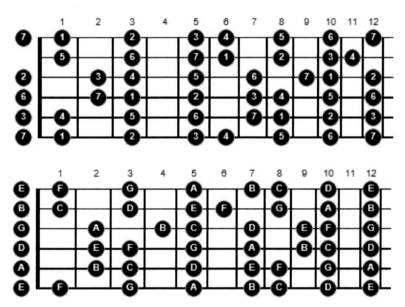

2. The Melodic Minor Scale

Allan refers to this as a D minor major 7 scale, and never once calls it the melodic minor scale, as the rest of us mortals would.

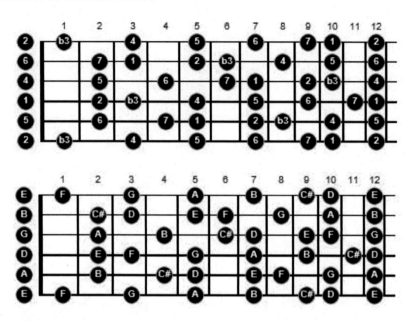

3. The Harmonic Minor Scale

In similar fashion to the melodic minor scale, Allan refers to this one as an A minor major 7 scale with a flat 6—in other words, the harmonic minor scale.

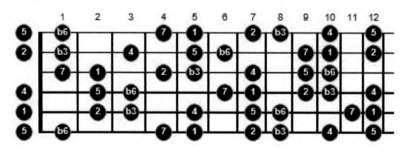

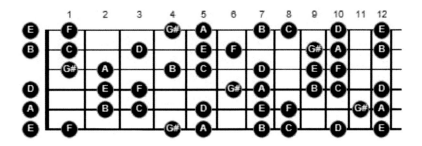

4. The Lydian Diminished Scale

There's an interesting discrepancy here as Allan refers to this scale as a 'minor major 7 with a raised 4th' which I would call the Lydian Diminished Scale. He then remarks that people refer to it as the Harmonic Major Scale, but that scale has the intervals 1, 2, 3, 4, 5, b6, 7, and in the diagram the intervals are clearly, 1, 2, b3, #4, 5, 6, 7.

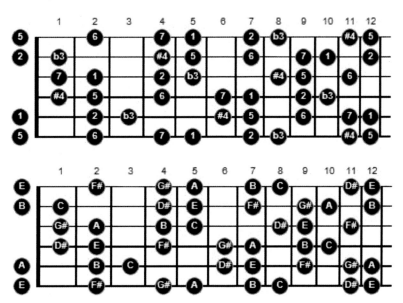

5. The Diminished Scale

Allan has another name for this scale but it's basically a diminished scale. In the video it's shown in Ab.

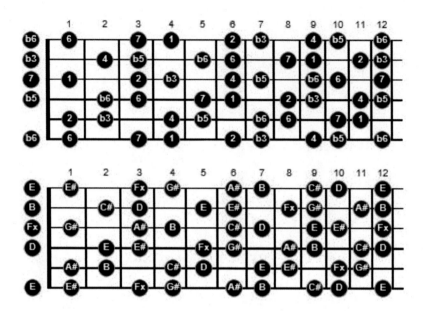

I imagine you can already see some familiar scale shapes popping out in the above patterns; even barre chords! The good news is that if the scale pattern contains the chord shape, the next time you're soloing over that chord, you can use the scale.

The remaining scales are basically major, minor and dominant scales with added notes, and are widely used in bebop. For the purposes of this book we'll concentrate on the first five scales as these are more than enough for a mere mortal if you take into account that we'll be extracting chords from these scales, as well as learning them over the entire length of the neck. What's more, as these scales are fairly common, they are much easier to incorporate into your own playing than the latter ones, and therefore much more usable.

Two Holdsworthian Diminished Scales

As we know, in Allan's system for improvisation and chord playing, everything is derived from the scale pattern in question. In this chapter, we'll look at two diminished scales: the half-whole, which means that we get a symmetrical sequence of notes starting in a half-step (semi-tone, ST) and alternating with a whole-step (tone, T), which gives us:

ST – T – ST – T – ST – T – ST – T – ST

And the whole-half, which is the same idea starting on a whole-step:

T – ST – T – ST – T – ST – T – ST – T

If you look at this the length of the neck, as Allan would, you can then begin to extract chords. Look at the following neck diagram for the C Half-Whole Diminished Scale and see what chords you can find:

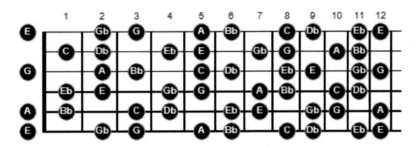

If you zero in on the C at the third fret of the A string, you should be able to make out the following chords: C, Cm, C6, Cm7, Cm13, Cm7b5, C7, C7b9, C7#9, plus a host of others, which means you can play the C Half-Whole Diminished Scale over... pretty much anything!

Obviously, you're going to a get a fairly outside sound over these chords, or, 'all the rude notes', as Allan would say, so you might want to use it sparingly, or not.

Look again at the pattern and you'll see that it separates into repeating blocks:

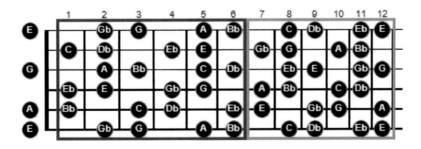

I imagine that Allan may have learned the scale this way given his liking of four-note-per string patterns, and he certainly would have had no problem with the stretches, even down at the nut.

If you want to break the pattern down into yet more manageable chunks, notice that it repeats every three frets:

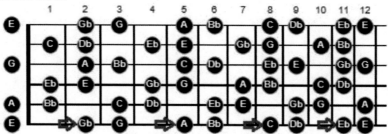

Now, all those chords we found from the C root note also apply to the notes marked above! This is one of the most versatile scales out there, and one of the most overlooked scales by guitarists. The symmetrical nature of the scale also throws into doubt the real root note as any of the above notes could theoretically be the root, but it doesn't really matter as long as you can pull out the pattern when you need it.

The Whole-Half Diminished Scale
You're going to love this. Simply shift the half-whole pattern down a fret and you get the whole-half pattern! Here they are together so you can see it.

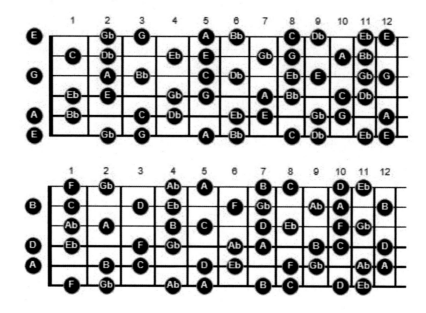

Imagine the fun you can have with this one! Do bear in mind though that when you shift the whole thing down, the chords you can (technically) play over change. As regards C chords we now have a CmM7b5, C6sus2sus4 (Dm7/C), CM#9sus4, and a host of other Holdsworthian chords. You could also come up with your own chords by finding groups of (usually 4) notes that you like the sound of and moving these sets of notes up and down the fretboard as we did earlier in the book.

Putting It All Together – How to Practice

Now comes the slightly tedious part of putting it all together. I recommend practicing in the following manner:

1. Choose a scale to work on.
2. Have the diagram in front of you.
3. Warm up with some 4NPS practice.
4. Play the scale from the diagram up and down one string; do the same for all the strings.
5. Practice 'juggling the notes around' by jumping to and from different parts of the fretboard, incorporate string skipping.
6. Avoid slipping back into CAGED and 3NPS patterns, <u>and make sure you're respecting the 'next note, next finger' rule.</u>
7. Use the mirror technique and practice the pattern from frets 13 to 24; imagine the guitar split in two sections.
8. Try to pull chords from the scale pattern. There are basically two types of chords you can pull out: 1) chords you know, and 2) chords you don't know. Both are valid as you know what scale you can use over them.
9. Find a four-note shape and move it up and down the fretboard in sets of notes as we did in a previous section.
10. Relax and improvise freely.

A Word About Technique

Allan is famous for his fluid, legato soloing and saxophone-esque tone. The key to adopting Allan's technique/tone is not to practice endless legato runs, but to understand the tone he's aiming for which is that of a saxophone or a horn.

It starts with the way he attacks the strings, and this is what everyone misses; what he doesn't want to hear is the sound of the pick hitting the strings, and the easiest ways to do this are, a) have the pick flat to the strings so there's no scraping when you hit them, and b) use hammer-ons and pull-offs as much as possible to avoid picking in the first place. Once again, the idea is to produce a note without the initial contact of pick and string, or by reducing it as much as possible; once you have this is in mind you'll see the necessity of adopting excessive hammer-ons and pull-offs, or extreme legato.

Allan's vibrato is lifted straight from classical guitar playing where you move your fingers and hand from side to side, not up and down as you would in rock and blues guitar playing. Allan does use the whammy bar from time to time but refrains from bending strings. I suspect this would sound odd in the context of the sound he's going for since horn players can't bend notes.

Putting It All Together – Making it Work

Let's say you have a fusion-type chord progression to improvise over such as:

Bm7 Cmaj7 | Cmaj7

Bm7 Bbmaj7 | Bbmaj7

By working from the point of view of scales you first ask yourself, 'Which scales do each of these chords belong to?'

You might go for their parent scales such as G Major for the Bm7 and Cmaj7 and Bb Major or F Major for the Bbmaj7 chord. What you may not realize is that these chords technically belong to easily another 50 scales! Or the other 98% of the improvisational possibilities. Holdsworth has ventured into that other 98% which is why he might play diminished, lydian augmented and dominant, harmonic minor, or very likely the harmonic major scale over just the Bm7.

In order to do this, you must know the requisite scale pattern all over the neck and see that Bm7 chord in there somewhere.

Look at the diagram below for the **F# Harmonic Minor** scale, and pull out any Bm7 chord you know.

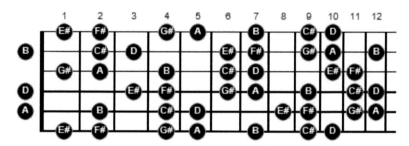

Now you know that **you can play F# Harmonic Minor over a Bm7 chord**—most likely it wouldn't have been your go-to scale, but this is what I mean by exploring the possibilities, and this is what Allan has done extensively. Incidentally, you can always use the chord technique to find groups of notes from this scale to comp over Bm7, or any other chord you might find in there. Mind-blowing!

Go through the same process for the other chords in the progression and you'll soon become aware of the immense range of possibilities available. At this point you can probably appreciate why I only included five of Allan's 10 Most Useful Scales! You can probably see some other chords in there such as Bm7b5, F#m, Dmaj7, C#dim, even a D7 cowboy chord! Use these chords to help learn the scale pattern by memorizing the notes locations (remember to avoid boxes or patterns).

Scale/Chord Reference Section

Use this section along with the previous one to begin to explore scales and chords. You'll find fretboard diagrams with both notes and intervals for the 5 scales covered. I've used the standard names for each scale, and recommend working through them from the same starting note as this way you begin to see similarities and differences faster. You may be tempted to think, 'What chords can I play these scales over?' But a better question would be, 'What chords can I find within these scales?'

C Major

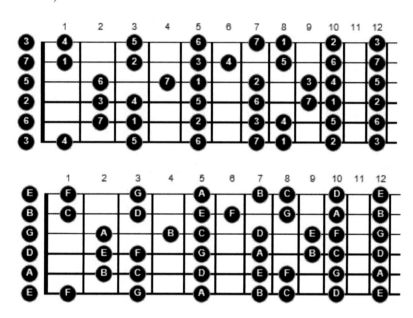

C Melodic Minor

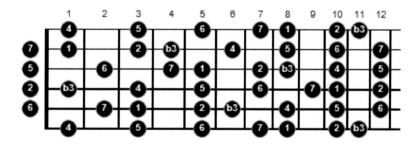

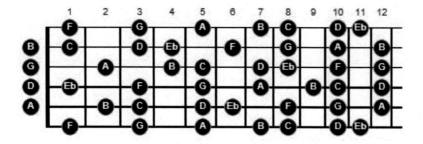

C Harmonic Minor

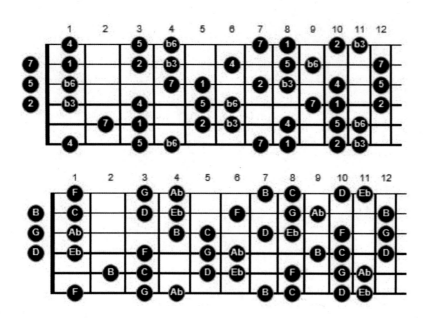

C Lydian Diminished

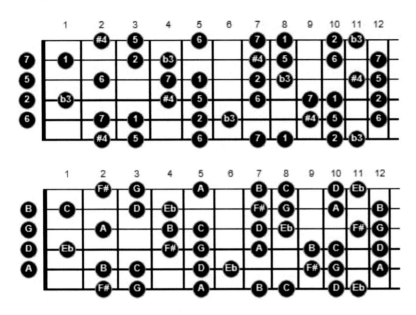

C Diminished

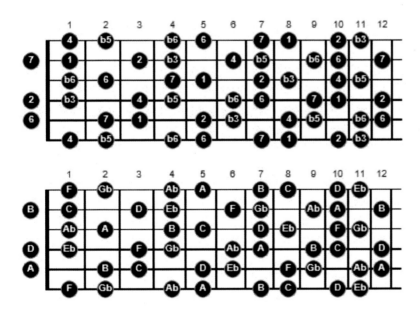

G Major

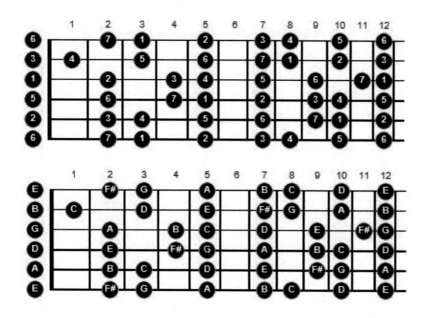

G Melodic Minor

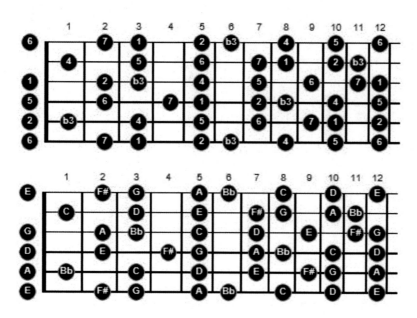

G Harmonic Minor

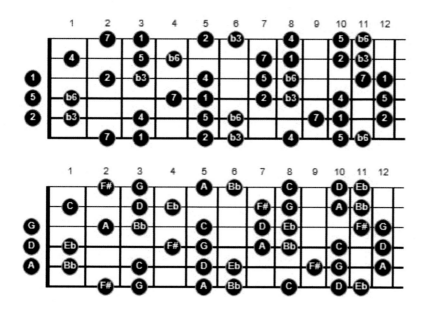

G Lydian Diminished

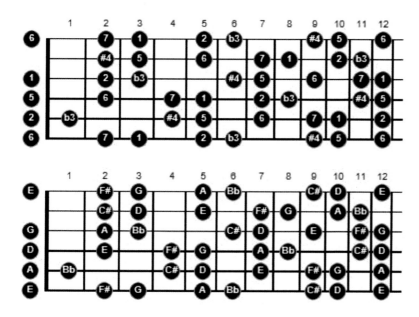

31

G Diminished

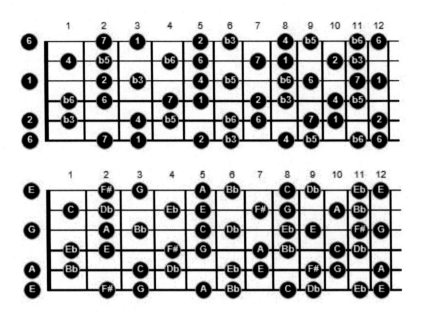

D Major

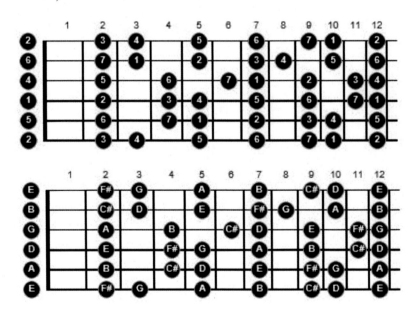

D Melodic Minor

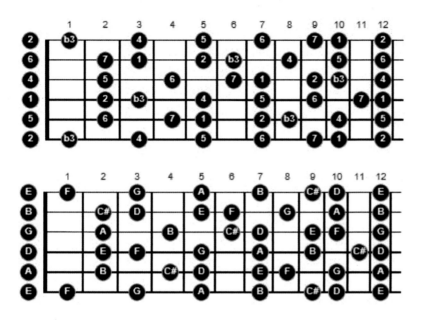

D Harmonic Minor

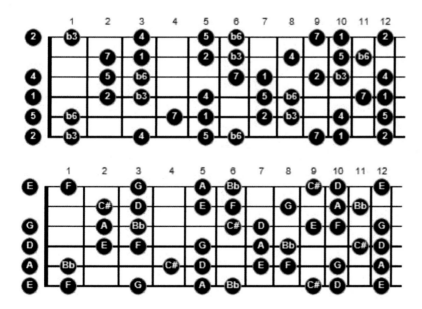

D Lydian Diminished

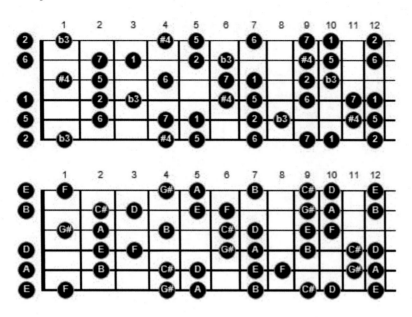

D Diminished

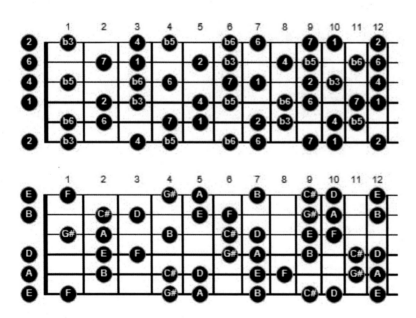

A Major

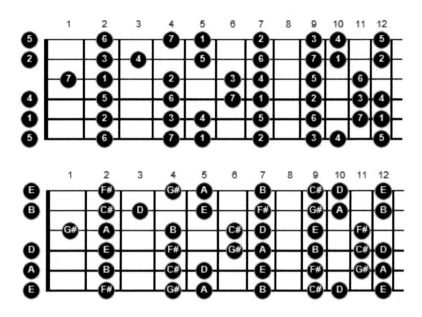

A Melodic Minor

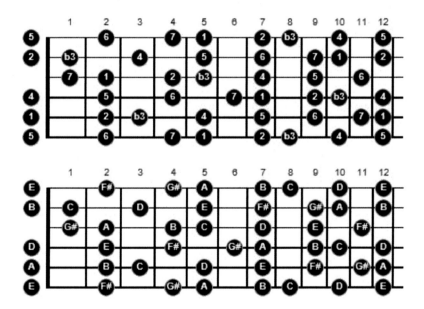

A Harmonic Minor

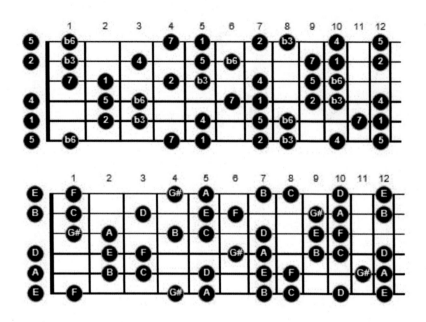

A Lydian Diminished

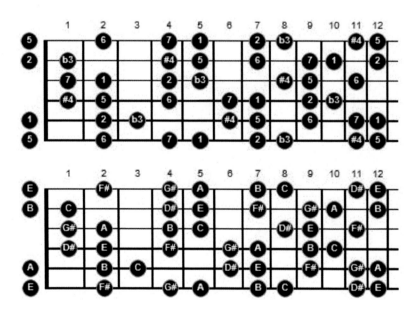

A Diminished

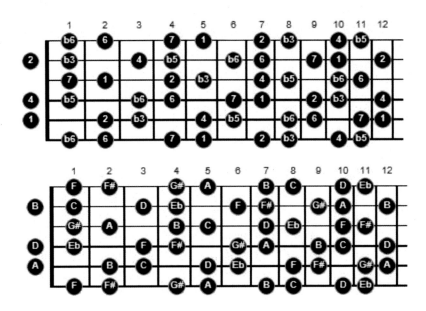

E Major

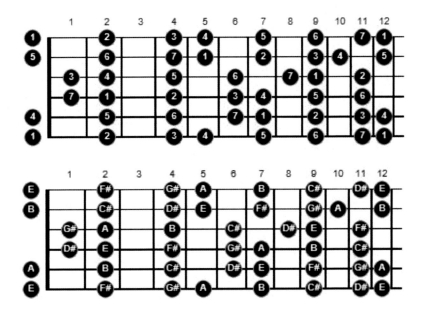

E Melodic Minor

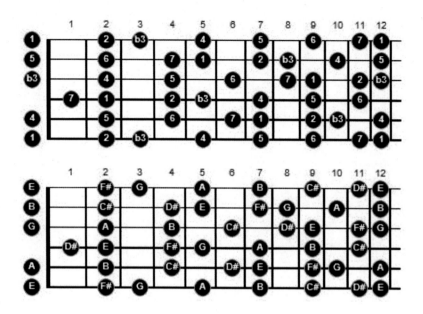

E Harmonic Minor

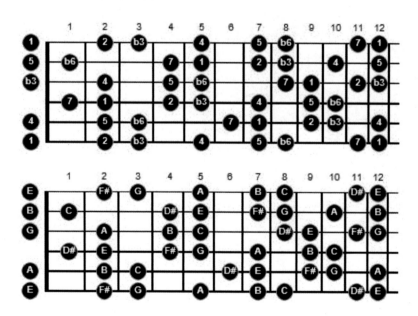

38

E Lydian Diminished

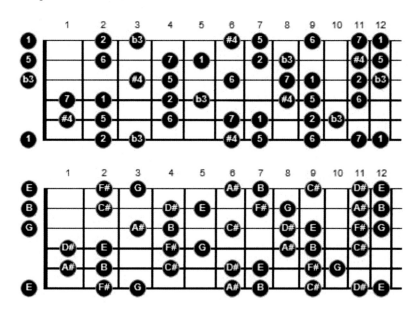

E Diminished

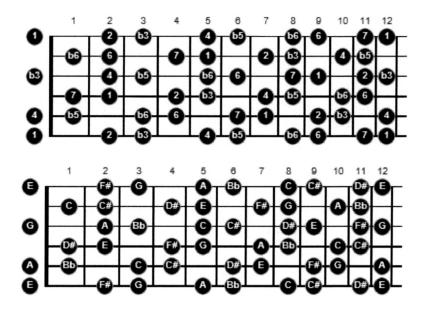

B Major

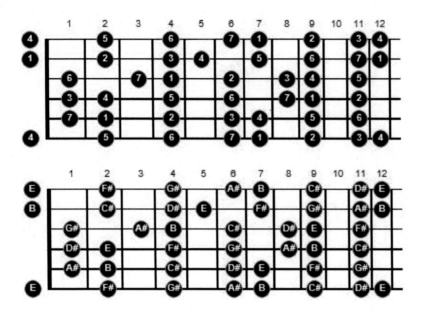

B Melodic Minor

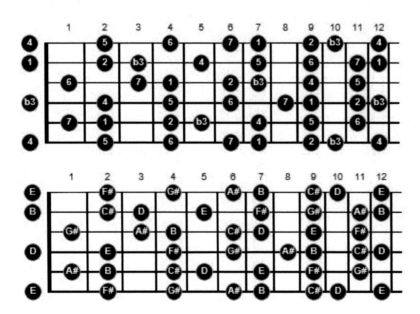

40

B Harmonic Minor

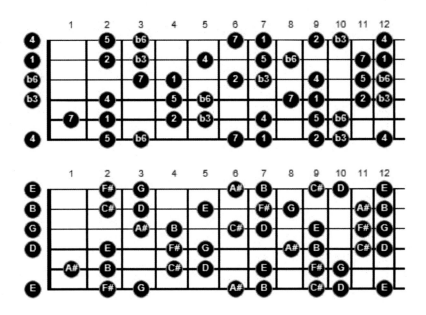

B Lydian Diminished

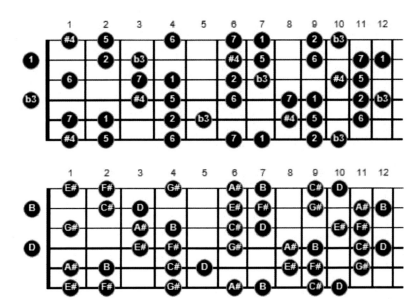

B Diminished

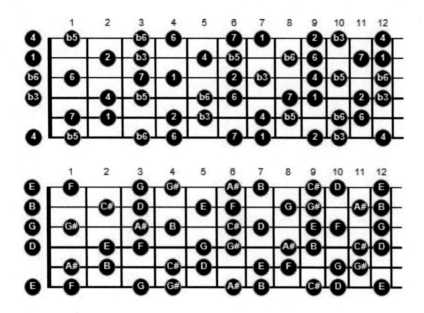

F# Major

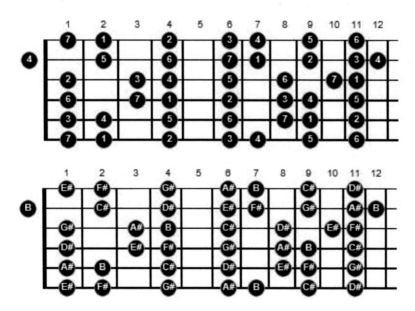

F# Melodic Minor

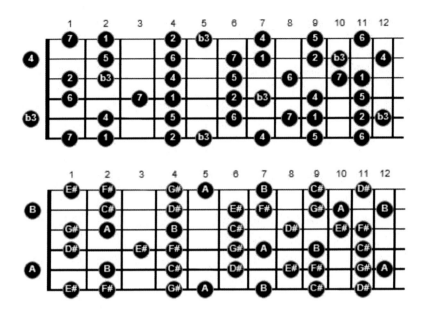

F# Harmonic Minor

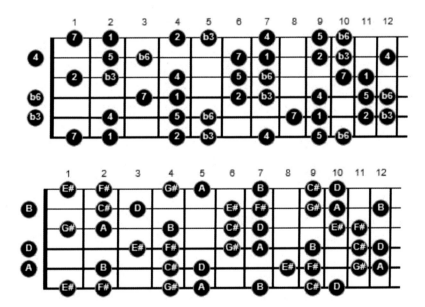

43

F# Lydian Diminished

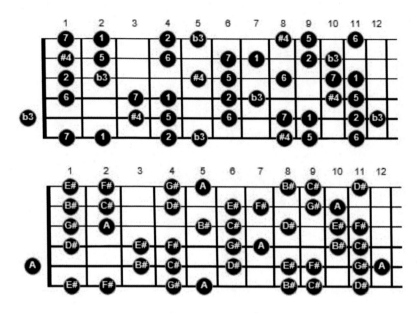

F# Diminished

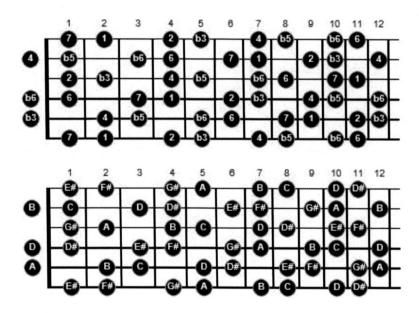

C# Major

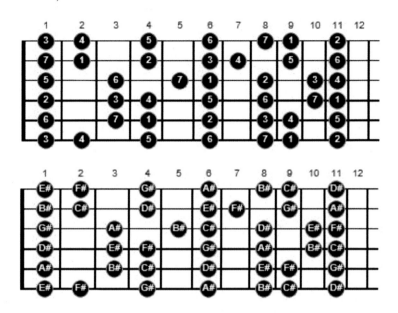

C# Melodic Minor

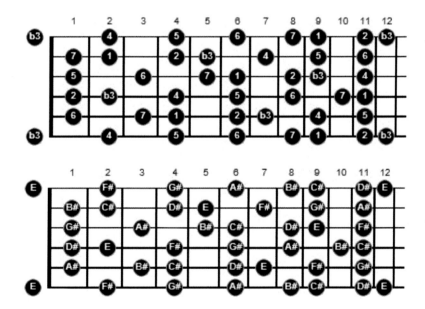

45

C# Harmonic Minor

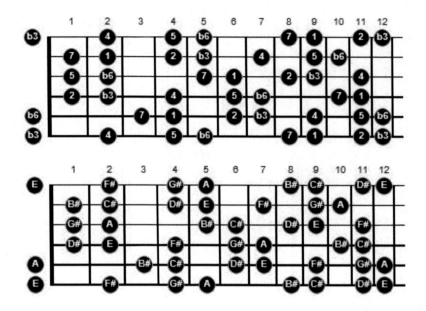

C# Lydian Diminished

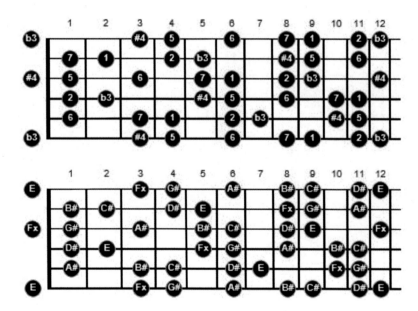

46

C# Diminished

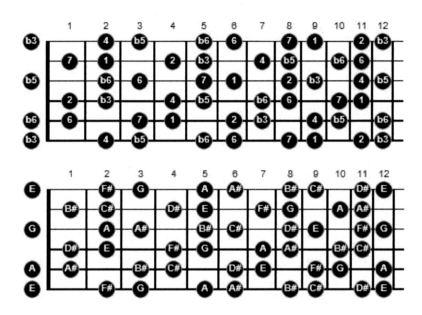

Ab Major

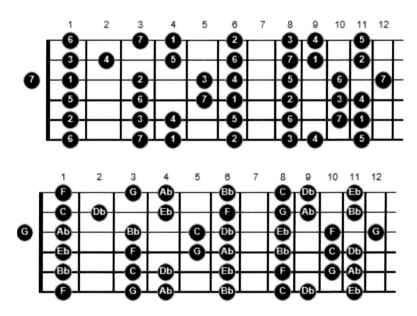

47

Ab Melodic Minor

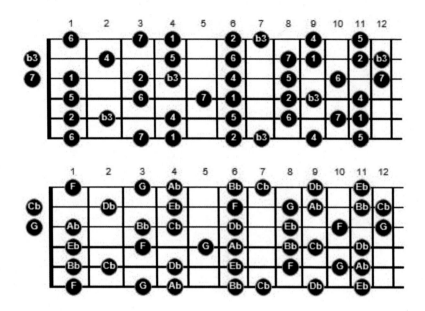

Ab Harmonic Minor

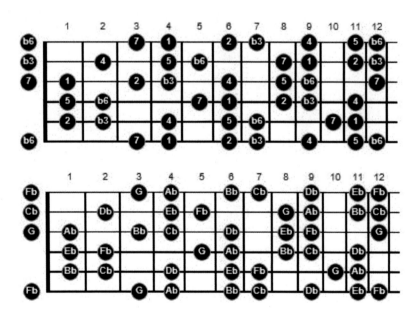

48

Ab Lydian Diminished

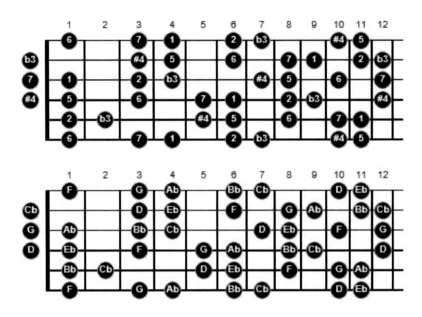

Ab Diminished

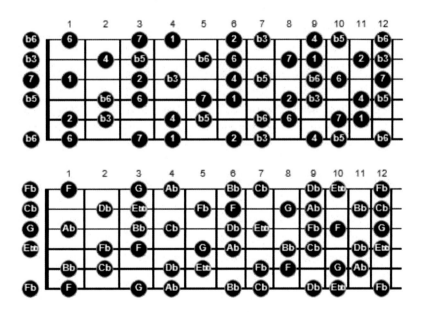

49

Eb Major

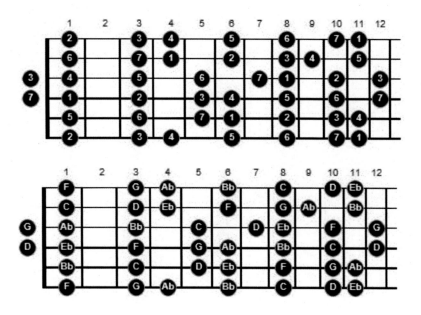

Eb Melodic Minor

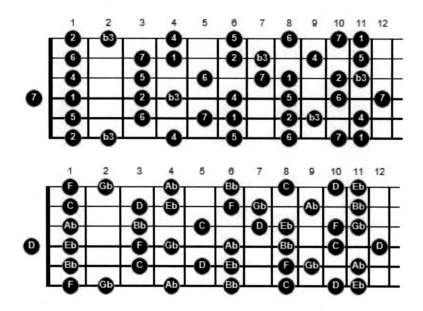

Eb Harmonic Minor

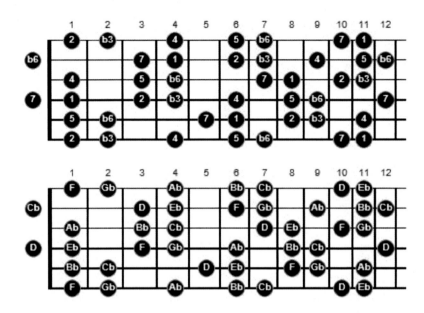

Eb Lydian Diminished

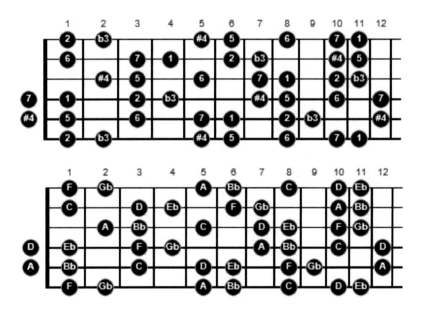

Eb Diminished

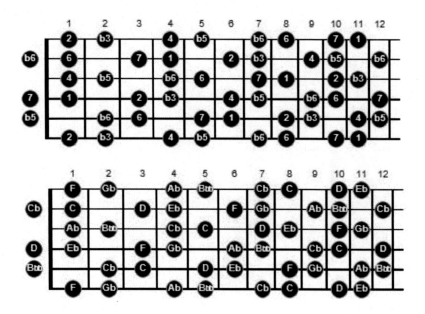

Bb Major

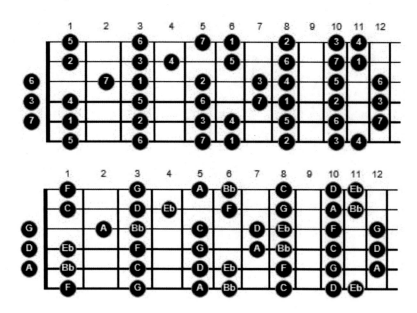

Bb Melodic Minor

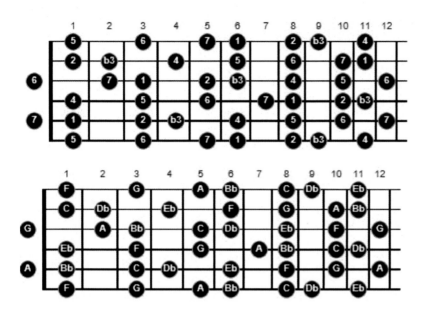

Bb Harmonic Minor

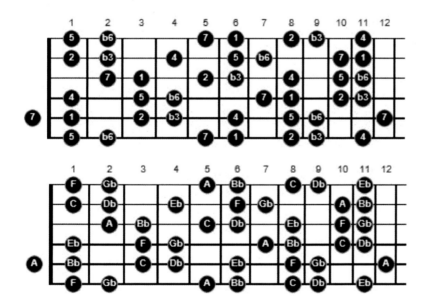

53

Bb Lydian Diminished

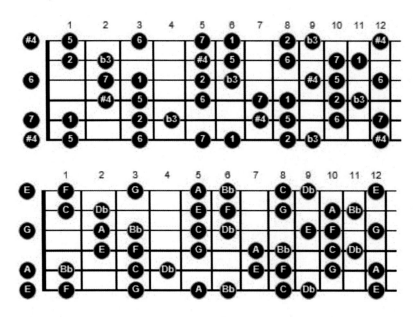

Bb Diminished

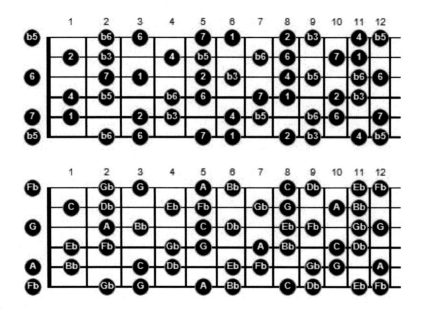

F Major

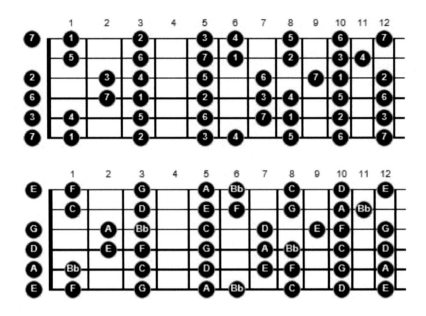

F Melodic Minor

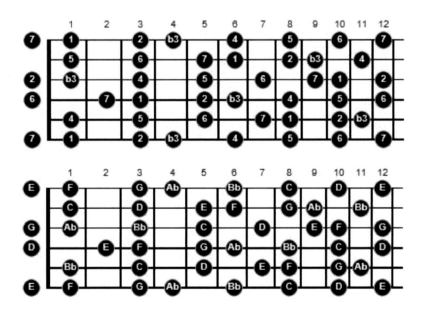

F Harmonic Minor

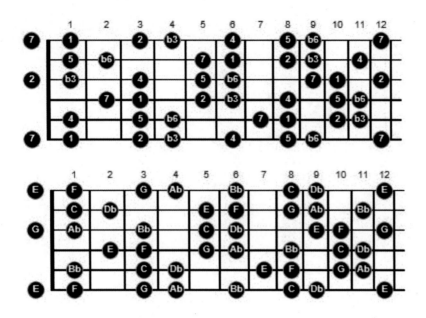

F Lydian Diminished

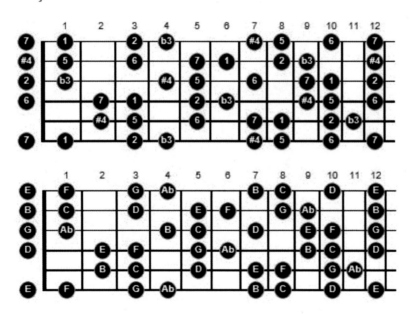

F Diminished

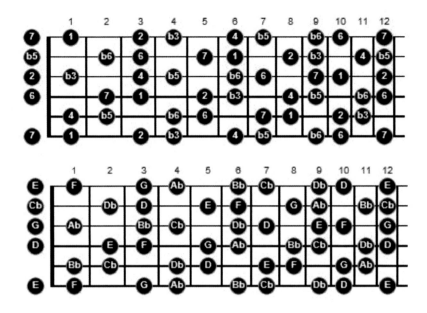

A Final Word

Thank you for reading this book. I hope it has given you an insight into Allan's playing, and that you've been able to make use of these concepts in your own playing. As you can probably now tell, there's plenty of woodshedding to be done here, but it is incredible rewarding when it starts to come together. By working through the scale/chord diagrams as suggested you're giving not only your hands a workout, but you're expanding creativity, dexterity and harmonic awareness on the guitar, and this can only lead to great things.

To your best playing yet,

Graham
www.unlocktheguitar.net

More from Unlock the Guitar

Visit www.unlocktheguitar.net for more insight into all things guitar on the **blog**, and our extensive selection of eBooks on scales, chords, and the bestselling guitar hacks series.

-Hacking the CAGED System – Book 1
-Hacking the CAGED System – Book 2
-Melodic Soloing in 10 Days
-The Two Position Scale System – Scales and Arpeggios
-50 Guitar Hacks for the Thinking Man's Guitarist
-50 More Guitar Hacks for the Thinking Man's Guitarist
-50 Guitar Hacks for the Advancing Guitarist
-Shred Guitar Mechanics: Fretboard Dexterity through 4NPS Scales
-Let Go of What You Know – How to Improvise Freely on Guitar
-Soloing without Scales
-Guitar Hacks: Triads and Inversions
-7 String Guitar Method – Book 1

12572153R00036